HOW TO MAKE
A Rainbow
Great Things to Make and Do
for 7 Year Olds

KINGFISHER BOOKS
Grisewood & Dempsey Inc.
95 Madison Avenue
New York, New York 10016

First American edition 1994
10 9 8 7 6 5 4 3 2 1
© Grisewood & Dempsey Ltd. 1994

Library of Congress Cataloging-in-Publication Data
Manley, Deborah.
    How to make a rainbow : 40 great things to make and do for
seven year olds / Deborah Manley. -- 1st American ed.
        p.   cm.
    1. Handicraft--Juvenile literature.   2. Games--Juvenile
literature. [1. Handicraft.   2. Games.]   I. Title.
    TT160.M2635   1994
745.5--dc20   93-23331   CIP   AC

ISBN 1-85697-929-6

Design and illustration by The Pinpoint Design Company
Printed in Great Britain

HOW TO MAKE
A Rainbow

Great Things to Make and Do
for 7 Year Olds

Deborah Manley

Kingfisher Books

NEW YORK

CONTENTS

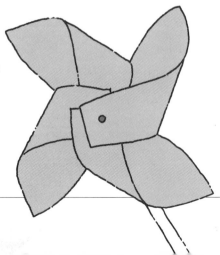

HANDY TIPS

Make a banjo out of a paper tissue box, or transform some old corks into a creepy-crawly caterpillar! With a little imagination, many types of household trash can be used to make all kinds of weird and wonderful things.

Start a collecting box ...
Keep your eyes open for possible materials and store them in a box or bag.

• Old Christmas or birthday cards and cereal boxes are a good source of cardboard.

• Old magazines, postcards, and newspapers can be cut up and used for collages and pictures.

• Pieces of string and yarn are always useful.

• Add old plastic bottles, buttons, matchboxes, corks, rubber bands, and toothpicks to your collecting box.

Tools to work with
Here are some of the tools
that you will need:

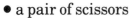

- a pair of scissors
- a ruler
- a hole punch and a stapler
- tape
- pencils, crayons, and felt-tip pens
- an eraser and a pencil sharpener
- paints
- glue—white glue works best for making models, but you can also use glue sticks for sticking paper and thin cardboard together. Remember to give glue plenty of time to dry.

Getting ready
Now that you have all the materials ready, you need somewhere to work.

- Always make sure you have plenty of room—a clear table top is ideal, but cover it with newspaper first.

- It is a good idea to cover yourself with an old shirt or an apron.

Cleaning up
When you have finished, don't forget to clean up.

• Put all of the lids back on your paints and on the glue.

• Throw away any pieces of paper and cardboard that are too small to save.

• Put anything that you haven't used back into your collecting box.

The ideas in this book are just a few of the things that you can make and do. Look around for other useful materials such as scraps of fabric and foil candy wrappers and try out a few ideas of your own!

FUNNY FACES

See how many different funny paper faces you can make.

You need:
a sheet of typing paper
a ruler
a pencil and crayons
scissors
tape

1. Fold the paper in half like a little booklet. Use a pencil and ruler to divide sides 1 and 3 into four equal parts.

2. Put some tape along the center fold.

3. Now draw faces on sides 1 and 3.

Draw hats on the top panel; eyes and noses on the second panel; the rest of the face on the third panel; and the neck and shoulders on the bottom panel.

4. Cut across the lines toward the tape on the center fold. Then move the flaps to make your funny faces.

Make your own band

Make your own musical instruments and get together with your friends to play them.

A box guitar

You need:
a large plastic box or a cookie tin
about eight rubber bands

1. Collect a variety of rubber bands; some thick, some thin; some long, some short.

2. Stretch the rubber bands over the plastic box or cookie tin.

Now your guitar is ready to play. The thick rubber bands and the longer bands will play lower notes, while the thin and short bands will give higher notes.

Drums

You can use almost any empty box or container to make a drum. But the best drums are those that give different notes because they have a drumskin stretched tightly over them.

You need:
a plastic bowl
a circle of plastic (cut from a plastic bag)
tape
a drumstick or spoon

1. Stretch the plastic circle as tightly as you can over the top of the bowl. Fasten it onto the sides with tape. (You may need some help to do this.)

PAY THE PRICE

In this game a bottle is spun to point at one of the players, who must then pay a forfeit.

You need:
an empty plastic bottle

The players sit in a circle. One of them is chosen to be the spinner. The spinner spins the bottle on the floor in the middle of the circle. When it stops, whichever player the bottle neck is pointing at must pay a forfeit chosen by the spinner. Once he has paid the forfeit, that player becomes the spinner.

Forfeits
Here are some ideas for fines: eat some Jello with your fingers; stand on your head; roll across the room; sing a song.

Tomato boats

You need:
a firm tomato
paper towels
softened cream cheese
a few drops of milk
a slice of cheese
some lettuce leaves
a bowl
a wooden spoon
a knife

2. Mix the cream cheese with the milk and fill the tomato halves with the mixture.

1. Cut the tomato in half crossway.

3. Cut triangles out of the slice of cheese. Set them upright into the cream cheese. Now your boats have sails.

4. Tear the lettuce leaves into strips. Use them to make ocean waves on a plate and sail your boats on it.

Cut out the seedy part. Stand the two halves face down on some kitchen paper to drain. These halves are your boats.

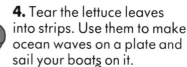

CHEESE SHAPES

Cut this cheesy dough into different shapes. Use an eggcup to make circles. Cut squares and triangles with a knife.

You need:
¾ cup all-purpose flour
¼ cup margarine
2 tbsps grated cheese
some water
a bowl and spoon
a rolling pin
a knife or cookie cutter
a cookie sheet

1. Put the flour in a bowl. Cut the margarine into little pieces. Mix them gently into the flour with your fingertips. The mixture should look like breadcrumbs.

2. Stir the grated cheese in with a spoon. Add the water, a little at a time, and stir it in until the mixture sticks together.

3. Roll the dough out onto a clean, floury surface. Cut out your shapes with a knife or cookie cutter.

4. Knead the leftover pieces together and roll them out again.

5. Place the shapes on a greased cookie sheet and bake for 10–15 minutes until golden brown.

NOTE

The oven should be set at 375°F. Ask someone to help you to put the cookie sheet into the oven and to take it out when ready.

GROWING BULBS

Buy some bulbs in the fall and grow some spring flowers.

You need:
bowls or containers
2-4 bulbs for each bowl
bulb fiber
water

Buy a selection of different bulbs, such as tulips, hyacinths, daffodils, and crocuses. You can mix them together in one bowl, or grow them separately.

1. Soak the bulb fiber in water. Squeeze it out if there is too much water. Lay some of the bulb fiber in a bowl.

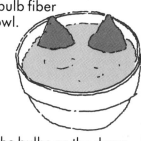

2. Set the bulbs on the damp fiber. Cover them with the rest of the fiber. Press it down firmly around the bulbs.

3. Put the bowl in a warm, dark place like a cupboard. The bulbs will need to stay there for about two months. Water them a little, but don't let them get too damp.

4. When shoots have appeared on all of the bulbs that you have planted, you can bring the bowl out into the light.

NOTE

Bulbs need water, darkness, and warmth at first. Later they need light. See what happens if you put some of your bulb bowls in a warmer place than the others.

A PAPER TREE

Make a paper tree. Once you know how to make one tree, you can make a whole forest.

You need:
thin cardboard
a pencil
scissors
glue
paint and a brush

1. You can make your tree any shape or size you like. Fold a "tree-high" piece of cardboard in half lengthways down the center.

2. Lay the cardboard flat on a table and fold both sides to the center crease.

3. Fold the cardboard over on these creases like an accordion. Draw half a tree on the top fold.

4. Cut around the tree. This will give you two identical trees, like these:

5. To make the tree stand up, glue one half of each tree to one half of the other tree. This will give you a tree with three sides.

6. When the glue is dry, paint the tree. Make it light green for spring and darker green for summer. Add red apples to it for the fall.

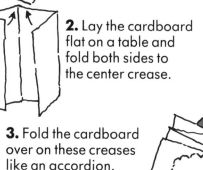

17

RACE DAY

Get together with your friends and have a race day in the backyard or in the park.

A three-legged race

You need:
a handkerchief or scarf for each pair of players

1. The players pair up and stand side by side. The left leg of one player is tied to the right leg of their partner. The pairs then race against one another on three legs.

Hop, skip, and jump
Racers move along taking a hop, a skip, a jump, and then a hop again. Anyone who breaks the pattern must start again.

2. Allow time for some practice running first. (It helps if partners hold on to each other around their shoulders.)

Handstand race

Players who can walk on their hands can race each other over a short distance.

All fours race

Get down on your hands and knees to race.

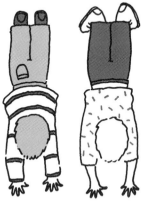

Walking race

Competitors must walk the race. They can walk as fast as they want, but must not break into a run!

Racing backward

Players stand with their backs to the finishing line and race toward it without turning around.

Aces low

This is a good game for about four players that will help you learn about a deck of cards. Aces are low and count as one.

1. One player deals four cards to each player. The rest of the deck is set aside.

2. The first player puts his highest card on the table, face up.

3. The other players place their highest card next to this in turn. Remember that some suits are more powerful than others.

4. The person who put down the highest card takes all of the cards and puts them in a pile in front of them. He or she has won the *trick*. They also put down the first card to start the next trick.

5. The player who wins the most tricks wins that round. To start the next round, deal four cards from the deck to each player. The cards that have just been used are put to one side.

Dominoes to make

Make a set of dominoes to take with you when you are traveling. This set is so small that it will fit into an envelope.

You need:
a matchbox
thin cardboard
a pencil
scissors
a felt-tip pen
an envelope

1. Trace around the matchbox onto the cardboard to make 28 domino shapes. Draw a line through the middle of each one.

2. Copy the domino spot patterns onto the dominoes with your felt-tip pen. The patterns are shown here:

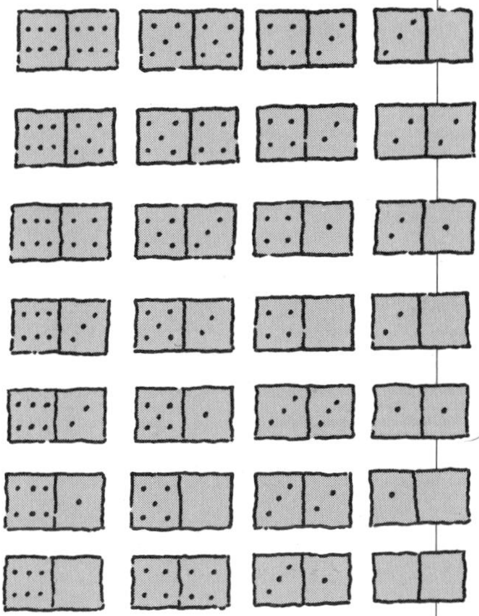

3. Cut out the dominoes and store them in your envelope.

BASIC RULES OF DOMINOES

Lay all the dominoes face down in the center of the table. This is called the *boneyard*.

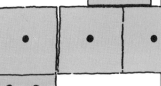

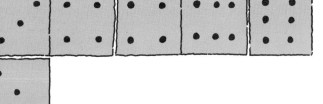

To decide who goes first, the players each draw one domino from the boneyard. The person who has the highest domino goes first.

Each player then draws seven dominoes from the boneyard and looks at them.

The first player lays a domino face up on the table. The next player has to play a domino to match it. If a player cannot go, they draw another domino from the boneyard. The first player to lay down all their dominoes wins.

On your own

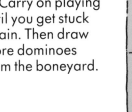

Here is a domino game to play on your own.

1. Shuffle the dominoes face down in the boneyard. Draw five dominoes and turn them over.

4. Carry on playing until you get stuck again. Then draw more dominoes from the boneyard.

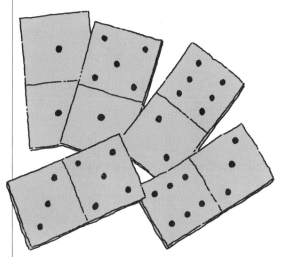

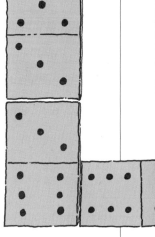

2. Play one domino onto the table. Then play as many of the other four as you can.

3. When you can play no more, make your hand up to five dominoes again by drawing from the boneyard.

5. Continue until you have played the whole set in your hand or used up all the dominoes and can't play any more.

FLOWERS
THAT LAST FOREVER

If you press flowers flat
and dry them, they will
last for years. It takes
quite a long time to dry
the flowers, so you must
be patient!

poppies

Choose flattish flowers
such as:

cosmos

anemones

impatiens

daisies

pinks

You can press leaves and
petals, too. Always ask
before you pick
anything.

24

You need:

blotting paper, tissue
    paper or paper towel
thick cardboard
heavy books or bricks

1. Pick your flowers on a sunny afternoon when they are completely dry.

2. Lay the flowers as flat as possible on a sheet of blotting paper. Put another sheet on top. If you want to press more flowers, add a piece of cardboard, then more blotting paper, more flowers, and another sheet of paper.

4. When you are sure the flowers are really dry, take them out very carefully.

Use your flowers to decorate greeting cards, bookmarks, and gift tags. Stick the flowers down with a dot of glue. Cover your cards and bookmarks with clear plastic film to make them last longer.

3. Place the flowers under a pile of heavy books or bricks and leave them until the flowers are completely dried.

NOTE

It will take a month to six weeks for the flowers to dry. Make sure the pile of books can be left undisturbed.

MY NAME IS ANN OR ANDREW

In this game you take turns using words that all begin with the same letter of the alphabet.

This is what you might say if the chosen letter were A:

My name is Ann.
My brother's name is
    Andrew.
We live in Athens.
And we sell Apples.

If the letter were T, the game might go like this:

My name is Tom.
My sister's name is
    Teresa.
We live in Toronto.
And we sell Tomatoes.

Each person in the game has a new letter for their turn. You can work your way through the alphabet. You can also play the game on your own, going from letter to letter.

CROSS IT OUT

Players in this game compete to cross out the same letter in the pages of a newspaper.

You need:
a page of newspaper
    for each player
a pen for each player

Somebody chooses a letter, for example the letter E. At the word "Go!" the players start crossing out all the letter Es on their page.
    Who can cross out the most Es before "Stop!" is called?

NOTE

The balance of text and pictures on the pages should be as similar as possible.

Flying birds

Make a flock of flying birds.

You need:

pieces of construction paper (in as many colors as you can find)
a pencil
scissors
glue
thread

1. Fold a sheet of paper in half. Draw the shape of a bird on it. Draw in the eye, the beak, and perhaps some feathers.

2. Cut out the bird, making sure that you don't cut along the fold.

3. Glue the two sides of the bird's head together and wait until the glue dries.

4. Then attach a piece of thread to each wing of the bird.

NOTE

You could be cutting out more birds while the glue dries.

5. Spread the wings apart slightly and hang your bird up to fly.

GOLDFISH IN A BOWL

Can you have a goldfish on one side of a card and its bowl on the other side and get the fish into the bowl? Give it a try!

You need:
a piece of thin cardboard
      about 3 in. x 2 in.
felt-tip pens
thread

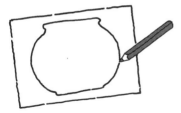

1. On one side of the cardboard draw a goldfish bowl.

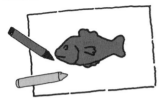

2. Turn the cardboard over, making sure that the goldfish bowl is now upside down. Draw a small goldfish.

3. Make two little holes in the middle of each end of the cardboard. Put thread through the holes and make two loops.

4. Now you are ready to put your goldfish into its bowl.

5. Hold the thread loops slackly between your thumb and forefinger, one in each hand. Whirl the cardboard around until the thread is twisted.

6. Slip the loops over your thumbs. Now pull your hands apart and then move them toward each other. Keep the action going in order to spin the cardboard. As it spins, the fish seems to jump into the bowl!

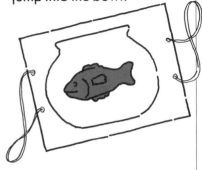

TRICKS

Amaze your friends by playing these magic tricks on them.

Brush off the coin
Set your audience this impossible task.

You need:
a coin
a clothes brush

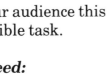

Lay the coin on the palm of your hand. Ask someone to brush the coin toward your fingers with the clothes brush, using only a simple brushing movement. They won't be able to do it!

Knock the cork
Challenge a friend to do this and try it yourself.

1. Place a small object such as a cork at one end of a table. Stand about nine feet away. Take three big steps forward.

2. Close one eye and try to push the cork over with your finger.

2. Now take your sheets of construction paper. Stick one of the date sheets you have made at the bottom of each sheet. Stick a picture above it. Punch two holes at the very top.

4. Each morning you can cross off the day that has passed.

3. Make a page like this for each month and put them into the right order. Thread a loose loop of yarn through the holes in all 12 cards and hang the calendar up.

Red letter days
Mark special days such as your birthday or your mom's birthday or Christmas in red on your calendar, or color them in to make them special.

April
1 2 3 4 5 6 7
9 10 11 12 13 14 15
17 18 19 mom's Birthday 20 21 22 2
25 26 27 28 29 30

33

RAIN OR SHINE?

In this game Sun and Rain compete to win the days of the month.

You need:
a page from a large old calendar
about 20 yellow counters
about 20 black counters
two dice

1. One of the players is Sun, the other is Rain. Sun throws the dice. If Sun throws an even number (2, 4, 6, 8, 10, 12), she places a yellow counter on the first day of the month on the calendar page.

Then Sun has another turn. If she throws an odd number (1, 3, 5, 7, 9, 11), it is Rain's turn.

2. Rain throws the dice. If he throws an odd number, he puts his black counter on the next day. If he throws an even number, it is Sun's turn again.

3. When all the days have been covered, who has the most—Sun or Rain?

NOTE

If there are more than two players, they can join in as Clouds and Wind. Each player then has 10-15 counters in their own colors.

Make a pinwheel

Wind makes the sails of a pinwheel turn. When you blow onto a paper pinwheel, your breath is the wind that makes the model whirl around.

You need:
a piece of paper about
  6 inches square
a strong pin with a head
a bead
a stick

1. Draw lines on the paper as shown and cut along the lines. Fold the corners marked with a cross to the center of the paper.

2. Push the pin through the middle of all four folded corners, so that they are pinned together. Thread the bead onto the point of the pin.

Now ask someone to help you to push the pin firmly into the stick. Make sure the pinwheel can spin.

3. Hold up your pinwheel. Blow onto it and watch it spin. Take your pinwheel outside on a windy day and see how fast it turns in the wind.

Icy drinks

Orange juice cubes

Make a cold orange drink using orange juice cubes instead of ice.

You need:
orange or other fruit
  juice
an ice cube tray
lemonade

Fill the ice cube tray with orange juice. Put the tray into the freezer. When it has frozen and you want a drink, put 3 or 4 frozen orange juice cubes in a glass. Fill up the glass with lemonade. As the cubes melt, the drink will taste more and more like orange.

Fruity drinks

You need:
pieces of fruit (such as
  strawberries,
  raspberries, and
  cherries)
an ice cube tray
lemonade

Put one piece of fruit into each section of an ice cube tray. Fill up the sections with water. Put the tray into the freezer. When you want a drink, put 3 or 4 fruity cubes into a glass with lemonade.

A WATER XYLOPHONE

Fill old bottles with water and make your own water xylophone to play.

1. Stand all the bottles in line. Fill the first one almost to the top. Put a little less water in the next bottle, and so on down the line. The last bottle will have very little water in it.

You need:
several glass bottles
    about the same size
    and shape
water
a metal spoon

2. Now your bottle xylophone is ready to play. Tap each bottle gently with the metal spoon. Do all the bottles make the same sound? See if you can play your favorite tune on your water xylophone.

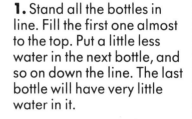

Keep a caterpillar

Collect caterpillars from your park or yard in early summer. Make a home for them and watch them eat and grow.

You need:
a shoe box
scissors
plastic wrap
tape

1. Ask someone to cut a window in the top of the box for you. Cover it with plastic wrap or another see-through material. Fasten it on with tape. Make some air holes in the side of the box. Now you have a home for your caterpillar.

2. Collect some of the leaves that you found the caterpillar eating. Put the leaves in the box and very gently put your caterpillar in with them.

NOTE

Shoe stores will often let you have a shoe box even if you are not buying anything.

3. Feed the caterpillar with fresh leaves every day and watch your caterpillar grow and change.

After a while the caterpillar will change into its *chrysalis* form. In this stage the caterpillar does not need to eat.

One day, if you are lucky, a butterfly or moth will hatch out of the chrysalis. When you think this is happening, leave the box open outside and let the butterfly or moth fly away.

Make a clock face

You need:

a circle of cardboard at
    least 8 in. across
2 strips of stiff paper
a ruler
a pencil
felt-tip pens
a paper fastener

2. Draw and cut out two
hands for the clock. The hour
hand is smaller than the
minute hand.

2½ in.

hour hand

minute hand

3 in.

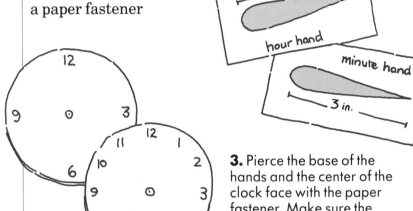

3. Pierce the base of the
hands and the center of the
clock face with the paper
fastener. Make sure the
hands will turn.

1. First write the numbers 1
to 12 in their places on the
clock face. To do this, mark
the center of the circle. With
the ruler, mark the hours 6
and 12 opposite each other.
Then mark 9 and 3 opposite
each other. Fill in the
numbers in between.

CLOCK FACE DICE

You can play this game on your own or with friends.

You need:
paper and a pencil
two dice

1. First draw a clock face showing the numbers from 1 to 12.

If you are playing with a friend, each player will need to draw his or her own clock face. Take turns throwing the dice and see who is the first to cross off all of the hours.

2. Throw one of the dice. Your aim is to throw the numbers in order from 1 to 6. When you throw the number 1, cross off the same hour number on the clock face and go on to 2.

3. When you have crossed off the first six numbers, start using two dice and cross off the numbers from 7 to 12 in order.

BACKYARD FAIR

It's loads of fun to hold a neighborhood fair in your own backyard. All you need are a few simple games for everyone to play.

Coin in the water

You need:
a bowl of water
a coin

Drop the coin in the water into the middle of the bowl. Competitors now try to drop other coins on top of it. The person who does so wins the coin.

Doughnut bobbing

You need:
two chairs
some doughnuts
string
a pole

1. Balance the pole between the backs of the two chairs. Thread the doughnuts on strings and hang the strings from the pole.

NOTE

You might like to raise money for charity by asking guests to pay a few pennies to play your fairground games.

NOTE

You might also organize races as part of the fun.

42

2. Competitors have to eat the doughnuts without touching them with their hands.

Guessing games
People have to guess as accurately as they can such things as:
the number of beans in a jar,
the length of a piece of string,
the weight of a cake.

Write down each person's guess. At the end of the fair, the person who was nearest to the correct answer gets a prize.

SCORE 10

Here are two more games.

Throw-in-the-box

You need:
cartons or containers
   of various sizes
some small balls
felt-tip pens

1. Number the biggest box 1, the next biggest 2, and so on. The smallest box will have the highest number.

2. Arrange the boxes on the ground.

3. Stand back and take turns throwing the balls into the boxes. Each player throws the same number of balls. Who can score 10 first?

Marble arcade

You need:
a cardboard carton
scissors
a felt-tip pen
marbles or small balls

1. Cut arches in the side of the carton. Write a score over each arch. Put the highest scores at the ends, the lowest scores in the middle.

2. From an agreed line, roll your marbles into the arches. See who scores 10 first.

BOWLING

Make a bowling alley with old plastic bottles.

Here are some other bowling games.

You need:
about 5 plastic bottles
a tennis ball
gummed labels
a pen or pencil

1. Line up the bottles from 1 to 5. Try to knock them over in order.

1. Write a number label for each bottle and stick them on.

2. Line up the bottles behind one another. Can you make all five fall down at once?

2. Line the bottles up next to one another. Stand about nine feet away and roll the ball to see how many you can knock over.

NOTE

Add up the score on the bottles you knock down for each throw of the ball. How high a score can you get in three throws?

BOW TO THE KING

For this card game you need two to five players.

Deal out all the cards in a deck. It doesn't matter if people don't end up with the same number cards.

First put your cards face down in front of you. The player on the dealer's left starts by putting her top card face up on the table. The next player does the same, and so on as quickly as possible around the table. When a King appears, all the players must bow, saying, "Your Majesty." The first person to do so picks up all the cards on the table.

When a Queen appears, the players must say, "Good morning, ma'am." The first one to do so gets the cards.

When a Jack appears, they must say, "How do you do, sir," and the first to do this correctly takes the cards.

When the Ace appears, everyone slaps it! The person whose hand is at the bottom of the pile wins the cards.

A player who calls or acts wrongly must pay a card to whoever played the last card. People drop out of the game as they run out of cards.

 # Shape fish

Before you can play this game you have to make your own cards.

You need:
30 cards about 4 inches by 3 inches
felt-tip pens or crayons

Decorate the cards like this:
3 with red triangles
3 with blue triangles
3 with yellow triangles
3 with red squares
3 with blue squares
3 with green circles
3 with black circles
3 with white circles
3 with blue stars
3 with yellow stars

The aim of the game is to get all three cards of one shape and color to make a set.

1. The players are dealt four cards each. The rest are put face down in a pile.

2. The players sort their cards into shapes. If anyone already has three of a kind, they may put them down.

3. The player to the left of the dealer starts. He looks at his cards to see what he needs to make up a set. He then asks any one of the other players for one card.

4. If the player he asks has the card, she must hand it over. Then the first player has another turn. If the player he asks does not have this card, she says, "Fish!" The first player then picks up a card from the central pile.

5. Then it is the next player's turn. Each time a player collects a set of three cards, he puts them down on the table. The winner is the player who gets all his cards down and has the most sets.

FOLDING FANS

Make a folding fan to keep you cool in the summer.

You need:
a strip of paper (about 6–8 inches wide and 16 inches long)
a strip of paper (¾–1 inch wide and 4–6 inches long)
glue

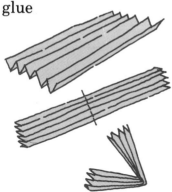

1. Fold the big strip into pleats, making each pleat about ½ inch deep. Now fold the strip in half.

2. Glue the small strip of paper around the fold at the bottom to make a handle for your fan.

A circular fan

You need:
a strip of paper (about 6–8 inches wide and 16 inches long)
a flat stick (like a popsicle stick)
glue

1. Fold or pleat the paper just as you did to make the first fan.

2. Hold the pleats firmly in the center. Spread out the fan at either end. Glue the two halves at the top pleat together. (You may need some help to do this.)

3. Pull the fan out the other way to make a circle. Glue the two ends of paper to the flat stick handle.

Fanning the fish

In this race you fan a paper "fish" along the course and onto a plate.

You need:
tissue paper
scissors
a folded newspaper for
    each player
a plate for each player

1. Cut one fish out of tissue paper for each player. Line the fish up along the starting line and put a plate for each player on the finishing line.

2. At the word "Go!" all of the players start fanning their fish toward the finishing line with their newspaper fans. The winner is the first person to fan their fish onto their plate.

49

More music makers

Add some more musical instruments to your band.

Banjo

You need:
an empty paper tissue box
three rubber bands of different lengths and widths

Stretch the bands across the hole in the box. Then strum away on your banjo!

Comb hummer

You need:
a comb
a piece of waxed paper

1. Fold the paper over the comb and you have your hummer!

2. Now press the hummer against your lips and hum a tune through it.

Sandpaper scrapers

You need:
two blocks of wood
sandpaper
thumbtacks or staples

1. Ask someone to help you fasten the sandpaper to the blocks of wood with thumbtacks or staples.

2. Rub the two blocks together to make a *sh-sh-sh-sh* sound.

Nail chimes

These nail chimes will make a high, tinkly sound.

You need:

about 5 large nails of
    different lengths and
    thicknesses
string
a stick
a metal spoon

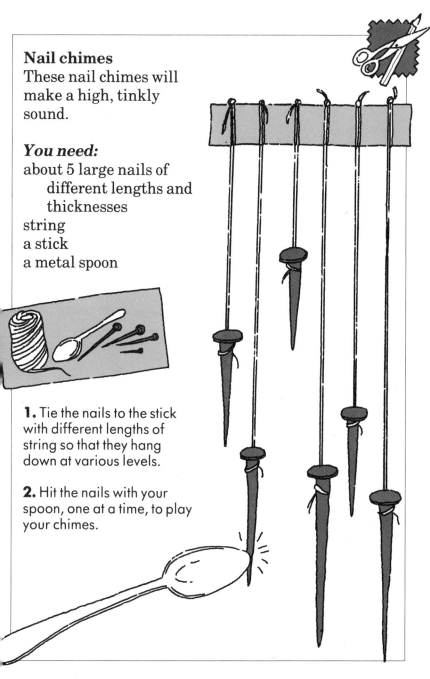

1. Tie the nails to the stick with different lengths of string so that they hang down at various levels.

2. Hit the nails with your spoon, one at a time, to play your chimes.

Making squares

Here is a game for two people to play on a long trip.

You need:
paper
a pencil

1. First you draw up a grid of dots on the paper, like the one shown below. This is your "board" for the game.

2. The aim is to be the player who completes the fourth side of a square. You do this by taking turns putting a line between any two dots that are next to each other on the board. The line can either go across or down, but not diagonally.

If you complete a square, you have won it. Write your initial in it. You also get another turn.

3. Try to stop the other player from completing squares.

4. The person who has their initial in the most squares at the end of the game is the winner.

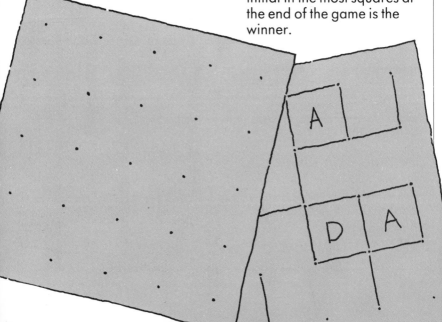

WORD MAKING

You need to make this game before you play it.

You need:
paper or thin cardboard
scissors
a ruler and a pencil
felt-tip pens
paper and a pencil for
    each player

1. Using the pencil and ruler, make 64 squares about 1 inch by 1 inch on the cardboard. Cut them out.

2. Using felt-tip pens, write one letter of the alphabet onto each square. Then write three extra cards for each of the following letters: A E I O and U. We call these letters vowels and we use them a lot. The rest of the letters we call consonants.

3. Write out two extra cards for each of the letters L M N R S T and H, and one extra card for each of the letters B C D F G K P W and Y. Now you are ready to play.

Make words
Place all the letter cards face down on the table so you can't see what they are. Each player picks up ten cards. In a given time (say three to five minutes), each player makes as many words as he or she can from their letters. Write the words on your paper as you make them. You can use each letter more than once, but only once in the same word.

The player who picked these letters

could make:

can
sack
bad
man
ran

bank
back
rack
cans
car

sank
cars
banks

Make a rainbow

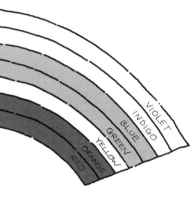

Every rainbow is made up of the same seven colors, always in the same order. These colors are: violet, indigo, blue, green, yellow, orange, and red.

Make a rainbow card

You need:
a circle of cardboard
paints and a brush, or crayons
a pencil

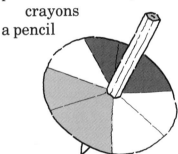

You have seen a rainbow in the sky when it's raining. But you can sometimes see a rainbow on a sunny day in the spray of a garden hose, if you stand with your back to the sun.

Make your own rainbow on a sunny day. All you need is a glass of water.

Stand the glass on a windowsill indoors, so that it just hangs over the edge of the sill. When the sun shines through the glass, you should see a rainbow on the floor.

1. Ask someone to help you divide the circle of cardboard into seven parts. Color each part with one of the rainbow colors in the right order.

2. Push the pencil through the center of the circle and spin the card with it. What happens?

Make a paper boat

All you need is a sheet of typing paper to make a paper boat.

1. Fold the paper in half and then in half again, making a crease in the middle.

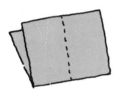

2. Fold the sides up to the center crease.

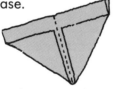

3. Fold over the open edges on either side.

4. Open this shape out and turn it sideways. Make the corners line up.

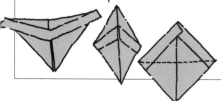

5. Fold the top corner down to the bottom. Turn the paper over and fold the other corner down.

6. Open up the middle again. Turn it sideways and press it flat.

7. The next stage is very tricky, so be careful.
   Take hold of the points marked A and B in this picture. Pull them out sideways. Press them flat.

8. Turn your boat right side up. It is ready to sail!

NOTE

Using a thin stick or a drinking straw threaded through a small sheet of paper, make a sail for the boat.

TADPOLES AND FROGS

When the first frogs' eggs, or spawn, appear in the ponds, collect some in a large jar. Be sure to collect some pond water as well.

1. Put the frog spawn into the pond water as soon as you reach home. A fishbowl or fish tank makes a good container.

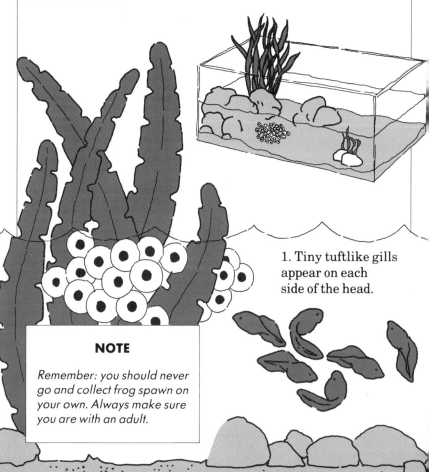

1. Tiny tuftlike gills appear on each side of the head.

NOTE

Remember: you should never go and collect frog spawn on your own. Always make sure you are with an adult.

2. Watch the frog spawn every day and see if you can see it changing. You might need to watch it through a magnifying glass at first.

3. When the tadpoles begin to come out of the frog spawn gel, put some pond weed and tiny bits of fish food into the water for them to eat.

Make sure there are rocks in the bowl for the baby frogs to climb onto. When they are ready to come out of the water, take your frogs back to the pond. There they will grow into big frogs.

5. The tiny frog is ready to come out of the water.

2. Two legs sprout near the tail.

3. Two front legs appear.

4. The tail gradually disappears.

SNIP-SNAP-SNORUM

This is a funny card game for two to seven players.

Deal out all the cards. Each player then sorts their cards and puts all the diamonds, hearts, clubs, and spades together. They arrange each of these suits in order, from the lowest to the highest (ace is low).

1. The player to the left of the dealer puts down any card face up and says, "Snip."

2. The player with the next highest card in the same suit puts it on top and says, "Snap."

3. The player with the next highest card plays it, saying, "Snorum." The fourth card is played with the words, "High cockalorum." The player who plays the fifth and last card says, "Jig."

4. That completes the round. The player who put down the last card starts the next round.

To begin with, the King is the highest card and the Stop card. It cannot be beaten. Anyone who plays a Stop card in a round starts again, as if it were a Jig card.

After all the Kings have been played, other cards become Stop cards. A player may put down as many Stop cards, one after the other, as he or she likes.

If a player has no card of the same suit to play, they miss a turn.

The first person to get rid of their cards wins.

HOW LONG IS A MINUTE?

You need someone with a watch that shows seconds to be a timekeeper in this game. The timekeeper starts the game by saying "Now!"

The person who guessed closest to the exact time is the winner and becomes the timekeeper for the next round.

1. Everyone has to be silent for what they think is 60 seconds —a minute.
2. When any player thinks a minute has passed they say, "Now!" The timekeeper keeps quiet until all the players have said "Now!"

NOTE

You can play the same game using the odometer on the car, trying to guess how long it takes to go a mile—or two miles. For this game you need to keep your eyes closed, as well as keeping quiet.

CORK ANIMALS

Make some animals from corks and sticks.

You need:
a collection of corks
toothpicks or
    straight twigs
straight pins

You may need someone to help you to cut the corks into smaller pieces. You may want to cut the sticks into shorter lengths too.

A dog

1. Put four sticks into a cork for the legs. Stick half a stick in one end of the cork for the neck. Then put a smaller cork or half a cork onto the neck for the head.

2. Add pieces of sticks for the ears and the tail—and there's your dog.

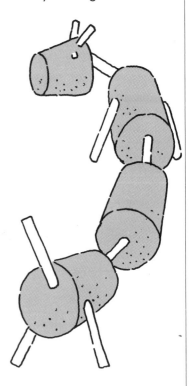

3. To make a long dog like a dachshund you need to fasten two or three corks together with sticks. Then put stick legs onto the front and back sections, and add the ears and tail.

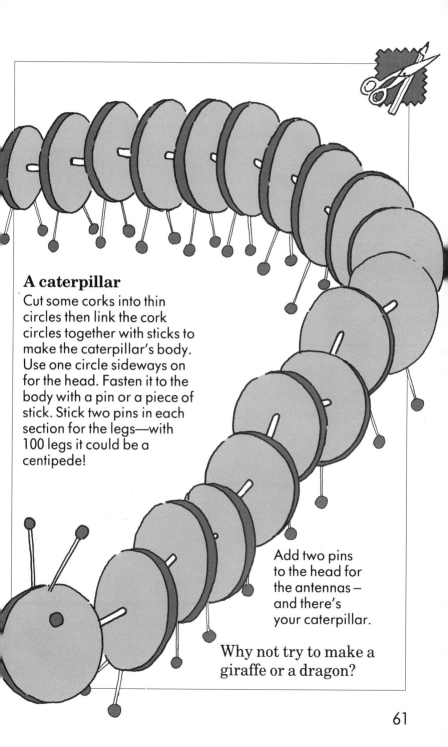

A caterpillar

Cut some corks into thin
circles then link the cork
circles together with sticks to
make the caterpillar's body.
Use one circle sideways on
for the head. Fasten it to the
body with a pin or a piece of
stick. Stick two pins in each
section for the legs—with
100 legs it could be a
centipede!

Add two pins
to the head for
the antennas —
and there's
your caterpillar.

Why not try to make a
giraffe or a dragon?

61

INDEX

Things to make

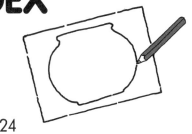

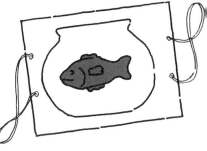

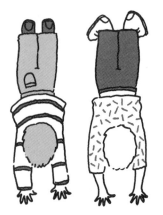

Action games for two or more players

Board and table games

In the kitchen

See how it works